10c/0
10/07

WORLD'S TOP TENS

The World's DEADLIEST SNAKES

by Michael Martin

Consultants:
The Staff of Reptile Gardens
Rapid City, South Dakota

Capstone press

Mankato, Minnesota

Edge Books are published by Capstone Press,
151 Good Counsel Drive, P.O. Box 669, Mankato, Minnesota 56002.
www.capstonepress.com

Library of Congress Cataloging-in-Publication Data
Martin, Michael, 1948–
    The world's deadliest snakes / by Michael Martin.
        p. cm.—(Edge books. World's top tens)
        Summary: "Describes in countdown format 10 of the world's deadliest snakes"
—Provided by publisher.
        Includes bibliographical references and index.
        ISBN-13: 978-0-7368-5454-2 (hardcover)
        ISBN-10: 0-7368-5454-1 (hardcover)
        1. Poisonous snakes—Juvenile literature. I. Title. II. Series: Edge Books. World's top
tens (Mankato, Minn.)
    QL666.O6M258 2006
    597.96—dc22   2005020096

Editorial Credits

Mandy Marx, editor; Kate Opseth, set designer; Jenny Bergstrom, book designer;
    Kelly Garvin, photo researcher/photo editor

Photo Credits

Ardea/Jean Paul Ferrero, 9, 26 (top right); Mary Clay, 24
Corbis/Andrew Bannister/Gallo Images, 16, 27 (top right); Anthony Bannister/Gallo
    Images, 29; David A. Northcott, cover; Joe McDonald, 15, 20, 27 (top left &
    middle right)
McDonald Wildlife Photography/Joe McDonald, 12, 26 (bottom right)
NHPA/Anthony Bannister, 23; A.N.T. Photo Library, 10, 25, 26 (bottom left), 27
    (bottom right); Daniel Heuclin, 17, 18, 27 (middle left), 28; Mike Lane, 4
Pete Carmichael, 6, 26 (top left)
SuperStock/Photocyclops.com, 22, 27 (bottom left)

Table of Contents

DEADLY SNAKES

Snakes attack when they feel threatened. Wouldn't you feel threatened if someone was about to walk on you?

The hiss and rattle of a deadly snake strikes fear in the bravest of hearts. For centuries, humans have dreaded the poisonous beasts that slither at our feet.

It may come as a surprise, but snakes are just as afraid of us as we are of them. Snakes will flee from humans if given a chance. But if a venomous snake feels threatened, we are in big trouble.

Each year, venomous snakes bite hundreds of thousands of people. Between 50,000 and 100,000 victims die. Even those who survive can suffer great pain and have ugly scars.

Experts disagree on which venomous snakes are the deadliest. Read on to learn what our picks are. All of them are dangerous. All of them can kill.

10

FANGS: Up to 2 inches (5 centimeters) long

HEAD SIZE: 5 inches (12.7 centimeters) wide

FYI: There are two types of gaboon vipers—one with horns and one without.

GABOON VIPER

Make the mistake of stepping on a gaboon viper, and it may be the last thing you do.

Gaboon vipers live in African rain forests. They are fat, heavy snakes with enormous heads. Their fangs are the largest of any snake in the world.

Gaboon vipers are hard to see. Markings on their bodies look like leaves or spots of sunlight on the forest floor.

When a gaboon viper feels threatened it makes a hissing sound. That would be a good time to back away. These snakes attack with blinding speed.

Gaboon vipers will only bite humans in self-defense. They will quickly jab and retreat. Even so, victims can die in as little as 15 minutes.

9 KRAIT

Most kraits are less than 3 feet (1 meter) long. They make up for their small size with extremely deadly venom. Kraits are among the most feared killers in India.

Compared to other snakes, kraits have tiny fangs. But kraits hold on and chew their prey to inject more venom.

Like many other snakes, kraits hunt at night. People are often bitten when they step on them in the dark. Kraits also crawl into sleeping bags and boots. How would you like to share your sleeping bag with a krait?

Krait venom paralyzes its victim's nerves. In worst-case scenarios, bite victims stop breathing and die of suffocation.

Female kraits lay six to 12 eggs at a time.

TYPES: 13 species of krait

HOW DEADLY?: Venom is 15 times more deadly than a common cobra's.

HABITS: Active at night

8

Australian brown snakes were once only found in the country. But they are becoming more common in urban areas.

AUSTRALIAN BROWN SNAKE

The culprit for most snake bites in Australia is the brown snake. About 3,000 people are bitten every year. Many victims can be saved with antivenom. But four to six Australians die from brown snake bites each year.

The brown snake's venom kills people in two ways. The poison thickens the blood, leading to heart failure. It also paralyzes a person's muscles. Victims die gasping for breath.

SIZE: 5 feet (1.5 meters) long

HOW DEADLY?: Only one other land snake has deadlier venom.

HABITS: Hunt during the coolest part of the day

7

KING COBRA

The king cobra is possibly the most frightening animal on the planet. At up to 18 feet (5.5 meters) in length, it is, by far, the largest venomous snake. These snakes can raise their heads 6 feet (1.8 meters) off the ground.

King cobras live in the jungles and fields of southeast Asia. When it feels threatened, a king cobra will rise up to face its attacker. It sways back and forth, making a deep hissing sound. The sound has been compared to the growl of a small dog.

King cobras can inject enough venom to kill an elephant. They also tend to hang on when they bite. In one reported case, an Indian woman was bitten while picking tea leaves. The king cobra held on to her leg for 8 minutes. She died 10 minutes later.

SIZE: Up to 18 feet (5.5 meters)

COLOR: Olive, brown, or black

HOW DEADLY?: One bite can kill any land animal.

FYI: Without medical treatment, bites are always deadly.

6 RUSSELL'S VIPER

Russell's vipers live in southeast Asia, along with about a billion people. Every year, tens of thousands of people are bitten by Russell's vipers.

Russell's vipers are quick and strike without warning. They uncoil like springs to pounce on victims.

Bites from this snake can contain twice the amount of poison needed to kill a person. Symptoms begin within 10 minutes. Death can occur as soon as 25 minutes after being bit.

The venom causes ugly blisters, internal bleeding, and kidney failure. Antivenom can save bite victims. Unfortunately, many victims live so far from a hospital, they die before getting proper treatment.

SIZE: 3 feet (1 meter) in length

OFFSPRING: 25 to 60 live young born at a time

HOW DEADLY?: Russell's vipers inject two to three times the amount of venom needed to kill a person.

Most snakes have larger scales on their head than on the rest of their bodies. Russell's vipers are the opposite.

5 PUFF ADDER

Puff adders take credit for 60 percent of all snakebites in Africa, where they prowl the deserts and grasslands. Puff adders hunt in the dark. Most people are bitten when they step on the snake by accident.

Puff adder venom kills by destroying blood cells.

Puff adders can strike from any position with incredible speed.

Puff adders fill their bodies with air and make loud hissing sounds when threatened. This is the only warning a person will get. Puff adders can inject enough venom to kill four people. But even people who survive their bites often lose a finger, an arm, or even a leg.

SIZE: 4 to 6 feet (1.2 to 1.8 meters) in length

OFFSPRING: 20 to 40 live young born at a time

HABITS: Active at night

4

Common cobras are exactly that in India—common.
People there must be careful to stay out of their way.

COMMON COBRA

Who doesn't know what a cobra looks like? Their hoods make them easy to spot. Not to mention, they are one of the most common venomous snakes in the world. Cobras are found in Africa, the Middle East, and much of Asia.

Cobras provide a public service. They eat mice and rats, keeping the rodent population down. However, they often creep into people's homes looking for a tasty meal. How well would you sleep if a cobra was hunting in your house?

Like other snakes, cobras would rather retreat than bite a human. But if a cobra feels trapped it will spread its hood and prepare to defend itself.

The venom cobras inject damages a victim's nerves, making him or her unable to breathe. Untreated, victims can die in as little as one hour.

SIZE: Up to 7 feet (2 meters) long

LIFESPAN: 20 to 30 years

FYI: Spitting cobras can spit venom, as well as inject it.

3

Saw-scaled vipers are small snakes that are hard to spot, making them all the more dangerous.

SIZE: 20 inches (50.8 centimeters)

HABITAT: Africa, India, and the Middle East

PREY: Rodents, birds, lizards, snakes, frogs, and insects

SAW-SCALED VIPER

Saw-scaled vipers are big trouble in small packages. These little snakes have bad tempers and are quick to strike. They are only 20 inches (50.8 centimeters) long, but saw-scaled vipers kill more people than any other snake.

Saw-scaled vipers are most common in sandy desert areas. They like to cover themselves in sand. Only their eyes poke out as they wait for prey. It is easy to accidentally step on a saw-scaled viper. They are nearly invisible under the sand.

A bite from a saw-scaled viper causes severe bleeding and fever. Without antivenom, most people die. In some areas, four out of five victims lose their lives.

Black mambas are actually grayish-brown in color. The insides of their mouths are black.

BLACK MAMBA

Black mambas are the fastest snakes on land. They reach speeds of up to 12 miles (19.3 kilometers) per hour. A race between a black mamba and a human would start out close. Luckily, the snakes can't move that fast for long.

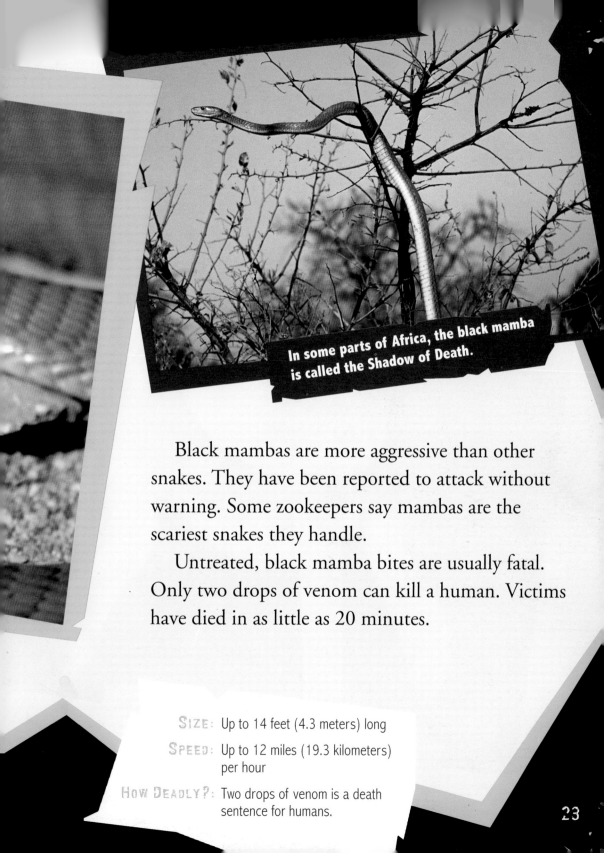

In some parts of Africa, the black mamba is called the Shadow of Death.

Black mambas are more aggressive than other snakes. They have been reported to attack without warning. Some zookeepers say mambas are the scariest snakes they handle.

Untreated, black mamba bites are usually fatal. Only two drops of venom can kill a human. Victims have died in as little as 20 minutes.

SIZE: Up to 14 feet (4.3 meters) long

SPEED: Up to 12 miles (19.3 kilometers) per hour

HOW DEADLY?: Two drops of venom is a death sentence for humans.

23

1

TAIPAN

Taipans are excellent exterminators. They eat mice, rats, and other annoying rodents.

Many taipans wander the dry flood plains of central Australia.

This Australian snake is the most venomous land snake on earth, and one of the most frightening. When taipans feel threatened, they try to flee. But often, they have lunged at people, appearing to chase them.

One bite from a taipan has enough venom to kill 100 to 200 people. Papuan taipans kill one out of every 100,000 people living in Papua New Guinea each year.

SIZE: Up to 11 feet (3.4 meters) long

TYPES: Three types of taipan—the Coastal, the Inland, and the Papuan

HOW DEADLY?: Venom is 50 times more potent than a common cobra's.

FYI: The first taipan antivenom was made in 1955. Before then, bites were fatal.

THE WORLD'S DEADLIEST SNAKES

10

GABOON VIPER

9

KRAIT

AUSTRALIAN BROWN SNAKE

8

7

KING COBRA

6

RUSSELL'S VIPER

5

PUFF ADDER

COMMON COBRA

4

3

SAW-SCALED VIPER

TAIPAN

1

2

BLACK MAMBA

UNDERSTANDING SNAKES

Snakes have to be captured in order to make antivenom. There's a job most people wouldn't want!

Deadly snakes are terrifying. But the fear they inspire is greater than the actual danger. In North America, you are far more likely to be struck by lightning than to be killed by a snake.

Deadly snakes actually protect humans. They eat harmful rodents. In the past, germs spread by rodents have killed millions of people.

Snake venom was never intended for people. Humans are far too big for most snakes to eat. They avoid people if given a chance. Just don't get in their way.

Glossary

aggressive (uh-GRESS-iv)—to act in a fierce or threatening way

antivenom (AN-ti-ven-uhm)—a medicine given to snakebite victims

fatal (FAY-tuhl)—causing death

inject (in-JECT)—to put a substance into someone's body; snakes inject venom through their fangs.

paralyze (PAIR-uh-lize)—causing someone to be unable to move or feel

prey (PRAY)—an animal hunted by another animal for food

venom (VEN-uhm)—a poisonous liquid produced by some snakes; snakes inject venom into their prey through hollow fangs.

READ MORE

Catala, Ellen. *Venomous Snakes.* Science Links. Philadelphia: Chelsea Clubhouse, 2003.

Crossingham, John, and Bobbie Kalman. *The Life Cycle of a Snake.* Life Cycle Series. New York: Crabtree, 2003.

Pringle, Laurence. *Snakes!: Strange and Wonderful.* Honesdale, Pa.: Boyds Mills Press, 2004.

Richardson, Adele. *Mambas.* Snakes. Mankato, Minn.: Capstone Press, 2004.

INTERNET SITES

FactHound offers a safe, fun way to find Internet sites related to this book. All of the sites on FactHound have been researched by our staff.

Here's how:

1. Visit *www.facthound.com*
2. Type in this special code **0736854541** for age-appropriate sites. Or enter a search word related to this book for a more general search.
3. Click on the **Fetch It** button.

FactHound will fetch the best sites for you!

INDEX